INSTANT POT
Magic

INSTANT POT Magic

50 Surprising Recipes for Beer, Jam, Bread, and More!

DAVID MURPHY

Racehorse Publishing

Racehorse Publishing books may be purchased in bulk at special discounts for sales promotion, corporate gifts, fund-raising, or educational purposes. Special editions can also be created to specifications. For details, contact the Special Sales Department, Skyhorse Publishing, 307 West 36th Street, 11th Floor, New York, NY 10018 or info@skyhorsepublishing.com.

Racehorse Publishing™ is a pending trademark of Skyhorse Publishing, Inc.®, a Delaware corporation.

Visit our website at www.skyhorsepublishing.com.

10 9 8 7 6 5 4 3 2 1

Library of Congress Cataloging-in-Publication Data

Names: Murphy, David (Cook), author.
Title: Instant Pot magic: 50 surprising recipes for beer, jam, bread, and more! / David Murphy.
Description: New York, NY: Skyhorse Publishing, [2019]
Identifiers: LCCN 2019001607 | ISBN 9781631584121 (hardcover: alk. paper)
Subjects: LCSH: Electric cooking. | Smart cookers. | LCGFT: Cookbooks.
Classification: LCC TX840.S63 M87 2019 | DDC 641.5/86—dc23 LC record available at https://lccn.loc.gov/2019001607

Cover design by Qualcom
Cover photograph by David Murphy

Print ISBN: 978-1-63158-412-1
Ebook ISBN: 978-1-63158-420-6

Printed in China

*This book is dedicated to everyone that has ever
encouraged me throughout my life.*

*Mom, thank you for starting me off in my culinary career and my obsession with
food and ingredients. It was your salmon patties that started this journey in my life.
You are so missed, and are gone too early from my life. You always believed in me
and were always my biggest cheerleader. We will forever miss you.*

*To my Stephen, thank you for your constant support, encouragement,
and side comments of, "But is it good?" You are my heart, and I love
you always. I'm so glad to be "stuck with you."*

*To my Jennifer and Angela, I couldn't ask for better sisters. I love my "scissors" so
much. I carry you in my heart. Thanks for eating everything I ever made!*

*To my Gigi, Stacey, and Tina, I love you all so much. Your love can
never be replaced. Tina, you are greatly loved and missed. You were
always so inspired to cook something in the kitchen, and we were happy
to be your guinea pigs, with open plates and forks in our hands.*

*Mama Eason and Daddy, thank you for always encouraging
and letting me know I can do anything.*

*Cheryl, thank you for the constant phone calls and always
bragging about me. I love you.*

*Sadie, thank you for being my constant cheerleader and second set of eyes!
I don't know if I would still have any hair left without you!*

*To all of my friends and fellow bloggers, I'm so very grateful to have you in my life.
I wish I had enough space to thank you all personally, but that would take up my
whole book. Please know how very grateful I am to have you all in my life.*

*Lastly, I would like to thank my Heavenly Father. You've never failed me. You've given
me the strength and courage to continue in life, and have let me know that I can do
anything through Your name.*
—Psalm 121

Contents

Introduction

I remember the exact moment that I fell in love with cooking. I was ten years old, and my mom was in the kitchen making dinner. As always, I was right there by her apron strings to watch what she was making. I'm sure I was always annoying her by asking, "Mom! What's for dinner?" However, she never shooed me away. She always took the time to let me know what she was making, and how.

So, what was this remarkable dish that I will forever keep close to my heart? Salmon biscuits with a cream sauce she made from scratch. My sisters and I lived for this meal. We were always excited when we saw our mom pull down the box of Bisquick and open a can of salmon. We knew the threat that we were about to indulge in.

I do have to let you in on a small secret: My mom was never known for her culinary skills in the kitchen. But after these salmon biscuits, you would have sworn she was the single most amazing chef in the world.

With this meal, I became obsessed by learning how my mom would take milk and transform it into a thick, rich sauce. It was that very special day of me watching my mom make her cream sauce, that I learned what a roux was. It was my very first food terminology, and I engraved it into my brain. It amazed me to learn what a roux was, and how it was a thickening agent for dairy products.

My family was very poor when I was growing up, so we always had to make food with what we had available and whatever the government welfare truck dropped off in our neighborhood. Normally things like long logs of cheese, yogurt, peanut butter, stuff like that. So we ate a lot of grilled cheese sandwiches—though we never complained about that! Melted cheese on seared bread with butter . . . is pure life.

Then I fell in love with watching all those cooking shows on PBS. Everything from *Yan Can Cook* to Julia Child. I saw this one cooking show where a lady was making a traditional Indian dish. It was green beans and red potatoes seasoned with paprika and other spices. I took a ton of mental notes and went to the kitchen. Lo and behold, we had everything that I needed to make the basics of the dish.

It felt fantastic to cook my very first meal that wasn't just warming up milk to pour over my Cheerios with honey drizzled on them.

Once I was done, I immediately pulled my sisters off to the side and "made" them eat it. They were younger than me, so they really had no choice. And they liked it! It was one of my first forms of encouragement that I received for cooking food for someone. I don't remember many other meals that I made when I was a kid, but the green beans and red potatoes will always be stuck in my head—it was the first meal I ever prepared.

It was my love for food and customer service that kept me in the restaurant industry since high school. Who knew that my journey would take me to where I am now? Now, I share amazing recipes, including Instant Pot recipes, and some life stories with my special needs sister and family, on my blog, foodnservice.com.

So, let's talk about my love and obsessions over my two children: the Instant Pots. It was two years ago that I was introduced the Instant Pot. I was like, *okaaaaaaay*. So what does it do? How is this going to add value to my life and cooking in my home? At first glance, I wasn't really impressed. All I knew was that I could "dump" food in there and cook it under pressure. I can't tell you the countless meals that I burned, turned pasta into mush, didn't cook the pasta long enough, forgot to add water, and the list just doesn't stop.

Did I read the manual? C'mon guys . . . No. I didn't read the manual.

There.

I admitted it.

One day, it dawned on me that I was doing this whole Instant Pot thing all wrong. I became consumed by learning how to work this machine properly and to my advantage. Instead of looking at the Instant Pot as an electrical pressure cooker, I decided to look at it as if I were using a wooden spoon in my kitchen—I use my wooden spoons every day when I cook. Why can't I use my Instant Pot just like that? I stopped looking at it as a nuisance, and became best friends with it.

The Instant Pot became my new "wooden spoon" of the kitchen. I cook a lot of meals in the machine, but I also use the machine as a tool to help me out in the kitchen. I tend to use it to cook a lot of side dishes, but then sometimes I'll finish up a dish in the oven to crisp it and give it that beautiful golden brown color that everyone loves.

Then I started thinking even more out of my little Instant Pot box. There are literally MILLIONS of different recipes that you can make in the Instant Pot. I wanted to make more than just "bland" colored foods. I wanted to have serious fun with it, and to stretch its limitations—I am doing new things with it every day!

That's what inspired me to write and create this cookbook. It's full of recipes that you can actually make in your Instant Pot. Some might be familiar, but I'm hoping there are a lot more surprises.

I'm hoping that this book will inspire you to actually pull your Instant Pot OUT of the box that it is still in. Yes, I know it's still in the box that you got for Christmas two years ago. You're afraid to use it, or afraid you're not going to know how to use it. I will no longer allow you to be intimated by this beautiful kitchen "utensil."

One of my biggest goals is to help you not be afraid of your Instant Pot. I want to introduce you to recipes that you've had before, but never thought about making in your Instant Pot, and to also introduce you to brand-new Instant Pot recipes.

I hope you enjoy these recipes as much as I, and my family, have enjoyed making them. Welcome to the world of being a "Pot Head."

Some Instant Pot Terminology

In this book, I'm going to be using a lot of abbreviations and terminology that I want you to get used to seeing all over the place, especially in online recipes and the Instant Pot Facebook community.

5-5-5: This is a common cooking method that all Pot Heads love to use for making hard-boiled eggs 5 minutes HMP, 5 minutes NPR, and 5 minutes in an ice bath.

Double-Boil Method: You're used to doing this on the stove top, well now we're doing it in our Instant Pots! To help ensure that your bowls or containers don't get stuck into your IP, use a thick piece of foil crimped onto the rim that the bowl is laying on, or use a big binder clip to attach to the rim of your IP.

HMP: High Manual Pressure.

Inner Pot: This is the metal pot that goes inside the machine. A lot of people call it the inner pot or pot liner.

IP: Instant Pot—*not* Insta Pot. Just to help clear up any confusion!

LMP: Low Manual Pressure.

NPR or NR: Natural Pressure Release. The Instant Pot has a pressure-release valve at the top of the lid. NPR means that you will NOT open the pressure-release vent. You will let the pot depressurize naturally. This process can take anywhere between 20–35 minutes, dependent on your recipe and your elevation.

PIP: Pot in Pot. This is a common cooking process to use with your instant pot. It means that you have ingredients that you're cooking in one pot, which then is placed on a trivet in your Instant Pot. I do a lot of PIP cooking in this book, and you'll see how easy it is.

Pot Head: An Instant Pot user!

QPR or QR: Quick Pressure Release. This means to open the pressure-release valve on top of your Instant Pot lid. It will only take a couple of minutes to depressurize. Once your pressure pin drops, you're safe to open your lid.

Sling: This is the process of taking a piece of foil and flattening it out into about a 2-inch width. You place this under the container or food that you are cooking in your Instant Pot. This aids in the removal of food from your IP. The IP can get really hot, and foil cools faster, which is easier to touch and remove.

Beer, Bread, and Jams

BEER

Makes 1 gallon

Before we get into the whole process of how to make beer in your Instant Pot, I wanted to make one thing super-duper clear: I am not a home brewmeister by any means. However, I've been curious as to how far I can take the true power of the Instant Pot and what else I can make with it.

In 2018, the world erupted as I made wine out of grape juice in my Instant Pot. People went crazy over it. Some liked it. Some loved it. Some hated it. Some use it for cooking wine. Either way, I was pretty ecstatic about the whole fermentation process and trying to get a nice and clean flavor profile from it.

It's with that concept that I began to consider making beer in the pot. I spent a few months reading about the beer-making process and freaked out a little. I wasn't too sure how I was going to make it work, and nevertheless, of how much money I was going to have to spend on everything to just have a failed experiment.

With a little online research, I discovered that companies make beer kits in one-gallon portion sizes. I was so excited because not only was this going to save me money, but it came with everything that I would need for the beer-making process, plus everything was already measured out for me. I love a no-brainer.

One last thing before getting to the recipe, please sanitize everything. It's such a key component. If you're using it in the beer-making process, beside ingredients, sanitize it. I think you get the hint.

Ingredients:

Beer-making kit (I ordered Northern Brewer Irish Red Ale, one gallon kit), mesh nut bag, and bottles for your beer

In the kit I ordered, I received:
1-gallon fermentation jug with cap and airlock
Mini auto-siphon and tubing
Bottle filler
8 oz. Easy Clean cleanser
Bottle capper and pry-off caps

Irish Red Ale 1-gallon recipe kit, which contained:
Approximately 1½ cups steeping grains
Mesh bag to place grains in
1 pound malt powdered malt extract
Hops (I had 7 grams. Each beer has a different level of hop flavors)
Dry yeast (I made English Ale)
Fizz drops (for bottling day)

(Continued on next page.)

Directions

1. Add 1¼ gallons of filtered water to your sanitized Instant Pot. Don't forget to sanitize your Instant Pot Lid! Press the Sauté button in Normal mode on your pot. We want to get the water nice and hot, not necessarily boiling. Sanitize your mesh bag and place your grains inside it. Be sure that both ends of the mesh beg are tied off securely.

2. Once your water is nice and hot, place grains in the pot and allow to steep for about 10 minutes. You can then remove the bag and trash it.

3. Place your hops in the mesh nut bag. A nut bag is very permeable and will stop the hops from disintegrating into the beer base. Add malt extract and stir till well dissolved. Then add in your mesh bag of hops. Lock the lid and close the vent. Place on High Manual Pressure for 20 minutes and allow to NPR. Be sure to press the Cancel button so the Keep Warm function doesn't keep the pot hot for a longer period of time.

4. While your IP is depressurizing, it's time to create an ice bath. I used my kitchen sink. I filled it up with ice and little water. Be careful when removing the metal pot out of your machine. You don't want to burn yourself. You want to bring your wort mixture down to about 60–70° F. This will take about 20–30 minutes in the ice bath.

5. Once the wort is cool, use a sanitized auto siphon to move liquid content into your sanitized gallon glass jug. Add your yeast to the jug, and gently rock it back and forth. This will help get some oxygen to your yeast. Place about a tablespoon of sanitizing solution into your airlock before placing onto your glass fermenting jug.

6. Once your airlock is on, place in a dark place. You will store this there for about 1½ weeks. Some beers may take up to 2 weeks, or even 3. It's very dependent on the type of beer you're making.

7. Bottling Day! Make sure your bottles and all utensils you are using are sanitized! Before siphoning beer into your bottles, you will notice that there is a nice layer of beer sludge at the bottom. When siphoning, try your best to not pour the sludge into your bottles. You will get a little in, but that's okay. Once bottles are filled to where you want them to be, place a fizz drop into each bottle. Lock your lids on your bottles, and then move to a nice dark place again. Consistent temperature is important.

8. Drink it up! After only 2 weeks, you can start enjoying your beer. It's refreshing, carbonated, and totally delicious. Have more fun and print up your labels for your private stock and share with friends.

INSTANT POT MAGIC

ROSÉ MARMALADE

Makes approximately 3½ cups

Everyone loves a great marmalade on pieces of freshly made toast, or even for baking thumbprint cookies. Adding rosé to the base of the marmalade adds an extra layer of flavor that makes your mouth rejoice. Don't worry, the alcohol cooks out of the marmalade—everyone will be able to enjoy this recipe no matter what their age!

I love how fragrant my home gets when I make this recipe. Your house fills with the sweet smell of strawberries with an undertone of vanilla.

A small note about this marmalade: You have to get it to the temperature zone 212°F–215°F. It's a soft-setting marmalade, but it will thicken once refrigerated. If you decided not to keep the whole batch to yourself, these make fabulous gifts.

Directions

1. To your pot, add all ingredients. Press the Sauté button and allow mixture to boil. Press Cancel and transfer marmalade to a storage container such as a bowl, and let cool completely. Refrigerate overnight or up to two days.

2. Strain and reserve the liquid, setting the strawberries to the side. In your pot, boil the rosé syrup until the temperature hits 215°F and the liquid is reduced by about half, about 15–20 minutes. The best function to use is the Steam function—it keeps a nice heat going strong. If you use the Sauté button, you might come across an error message of "HOT" which means that it's overheating and will turn off automatically.

3. Carefully add the strawberries to the syrup and continue to boil, stirring frequently, until the mixture is thick, about 25–30 minutes. Check the temperature regularly. This marmalade has a soft set, so it will be ready at 212°F–215°F.

4. Remove the vanilla bean and pour strawberry content into jars. A canning funnel will work best. Seal with lids and place in the fridge to cool.

Ingredients

4 pounds room-temperature strawberries (halved)

2½ cups sugar

1 bottle decent rosé

Juice of 1 lemon

1 vanilla bean, split and seeded

EVERYDAY PEACH SALSA

Makes approximately 3 pints

As a Georgia boy, I can tell you that I approve of this salsa! There is nothing better than cooking with deliciously ripe peaches, and then using them in a fun way. The peaches add just the right amount of sweetness that will slap your face with a smile.

Directions

1. Add all ingredients except pectin into your pot and press the Sauté button. Bring to a boil, and stir in pectin.

2. Boil for 1 minute, stirring constantly. Press Cancel and allow salsa to sit for 5–10 minutes to allow to cool.

3. Transfer to jars, seal the lids, and place in the fridge to cool. Peach salsa for days!

Ingredients

6 cups fresh peaches, peeled, pitted, and chopped
½ cup Vidalia sweet onion, chopped
½ cup red onion, chopped
½ cup red bell pepper, chopped
4 jalapeño peppers, minced
¼ cup chopped fresh cilantro
3 cloves garlic, minced
½ teaspoon ground cumin
1 tablespoon distilled white vinegar
1 teaspoon lime juice
1 teaspoon grated lime zest
1 package light fruit pectin crystals

You'll Need

3 1-pint sterilized canning jars and lids

JALAPEÑO PEACH JAM

Makes approximately 6½ pints

This peach jam is the right amount of spice you need to liven up your morning breakfast routine. You can add it to toast, cream of wheat, oatmeal, a muffin, and so much more.

Directions

1. Add all ingredients to your pot. Press the Sauté button and allow mixture to boil.

2. As the ingredients heat up, gently mash the peaches with a potato masher. Of course, if you want a smoother consistency, you can use an immersion blender. Press the Cancel button and wait 5 minutes.

3. Press the Steam button and bring your jam to a boil for about 8–12 minutes. Stir very often so it doesn't burn the bottom of your pot. If you want it a little thicker, continue to boil.

4. Press Cancel once you have your desired consistency. Pour contents into your favorite canning jars.

Ingredients

8–9 ripe peaches, peeled, pitted, and roughly chopped

2 jalapeño peppers, finely chopped or sliced

3 tablespoons lemon juice

1 tablespoon apple cider vinegar

5 cups sugar

½ teaspoon lemon zest

½ teaspoon grated ginger

3 tablespoons powdered pectin

KNEE-SLAPPIN' BACON JAM

Makes approximately 2 cups

Bacon jam is one of those necessary staples that you have to have in your home. It's great on burgers, grilled cheese sandwiches, or just by itself. My bacon jam packs so much flavor in a small container. You'll have people begging you to make this for them all the time. Get ready to become best friends with your Instant Pot.

Directions

1. Put bacon in your Instant Pot. Select Sauté and adjust to Normal. Cook and stir until bacon is almost crisp. Press Cancel and remove bacon pieces to paper towel. Remove bacon grease from pot.

2. Select Sauté and adjust to Normal. Add butter. Once melted, add onions, garlic, and horseradish. Cook and stir for 5 minutes until just tender. Press Cancel.

3. Add brown sugar, apple cider vinegar, instant coffee, cooked bacon, and water. Stir to combine. Secure the lid on the pot. Close the valve. Cook on High Manual Pressure for 10 minutes.

4. QPR the pressure. Remove lid. Use an immersion blender to break down ingredients to jam consistency. If you prefer it thicker, cook an additional 4 minutes on Sauté setting to reduce the liquid.

Ingredients

1 pound thick-cut bacon, diced into ½-inch pieces

1 tablespoon salted butter

3 large onions, halved and thinly sliced (about 4 cups)

1 tablespoon minced garlic

1 tablespoon horseradish

½ cup packed brown sugar

½ cup apple cider vinegar

1 tablespoon instant coffee

½ cup water

BOSTON BROWN BREAD

Makes 3 loaves

This was one of my favorite things to eat when I was a child. This is a close cousin of the date nut bread my mom used to make every year for Christmas; it brings back so many warm moments in a single bite.

Yes, I used actual cans (that I saved) to make these in. They were the perfect size, and you can use them for other Instant Pot recipes too.

Directions

1. Cream together butter and sugar. Add egg and molasses and mix well. Sift in the flours, salt, baking soda, and baking powder. As you add dry ingredients, alternate with the milk. Once done, fold in the mixed dried fruits.

2. Spray down the inside of the cans and the inside of the pieces of foil with nonstick spray. Evenly distribute the dough between the cans. Fill them up about 80 percent of the way. Leave about a ½-inch space from the top. Place the pieces of foil on top of the cans, lightly. We are just stopping excess moisture from entering the can.

3. Add 2 cups of water to your pot, and then insert the trivet into the bottom. Add the cans of dough. Lock the lid and close the vent. Cook on High Manual Pressure for 45 minutes and allow to NPR.

4. Allow to cool then remove from can to serve.

Ingredients

2 tablespoons butter, softened
¼ cup sugar
1 large egg, beaten
½ cup dark molasses
2 cups sprouted whole wheat flour
1 cup whole wheat baking flour
½ teaspoon salt
1 teaspoon baking soda
½ teaspoon baking powder
1 cup milk
½ cup dried fruits, like dates, raisins, cranberries, and currants
Nonstick spray
2 cups water

You'll Need

3 (15.25 ounce) cans (wash and save your soup cans!)
Aluminum foil that has been shaped in the form of the cans (to be used as lids)

RUSTIC BREAD

Makes 1 loaf

With this recipe, we are actually going to be using the Instant Pot as a bread proofer for our dough! This is a great staple bread recipe that you can use for your morning avocado toast, or side with your favorite seafood bouillabaisse. The texture is just perfect.

Directions

1. In a large bowl, add all ingredients and mix well. Turn onto a piece of parchment paper. Place in your pot. Press Yogurt setting for 3½–4 hours.

2. Preheat oven to 425 degrees F.

3. Time to remove dough. Your dough is going to be tacky! You will need to use floured hands. Remove dough from pot, peel off parchment paper, and place on a lightly floured surface. You want to form a nice ball shape. Dust it with flour, and cut a few slices in it with a sharp knife to add a little design to the top.

4. Place on a baking sheet, or place in a preheated Dutch oven. Then bake in the oven for approximately 25 minutes, or until a golden brown color. Remove from oven and allow to cool.

Ingredients

2 cups all-purpose flour
1 cup white whole wheat flour
2 teaspoons sea salt
½ teaspoon fast-acting yeast
1½ cups lukewarm water

You'll Need

Parchment paper

JALAPEÑO BACON CORN BREAD

Makes 1 loaf

Almost everyone I know loves corn bread, and who would have thought that it would turn out so moist and delicious in the Instant Pot? This is another one of those recipes where after it comes out of the IP, I place it in the oven to finish it off. This will go great with any meal, soup, stew, or just a little snack during the day. You should try this with the Jalapeño Peach Jam (page 9)!

Directions

1. Add 1 cup of water to the Pot and place trivet into bottom. Grease and lightly coat a 7-inch cake pan with just a bit of cornmeal.

2. In a large mixing bowl, combine the 1 cup cornmeal, flour, baking powder, and salt. Mix well with a whisk.

3. Add the grated cheese, chopped jalapeño, creamed corn, and scallions to the flour mixture. Mix gently until well coated.

4. In a separate bowl, whisk together the buttermilk, melted butter, honey, and eggs. Pour over mixed dry ingredients and stir until just combined. Once combined, add bacon and gently fold into corn bread mixture.

5. Pour into your cake pan. Cover the cake pan with a piece of aluminum foil. Place the cake pan on the trivet. Lock lid and close vent. Cook on High Manual Pressure for 24 minutes with NPR. Then place under a broiler for 2 minutes to brown the top.

Ingredients

1 cup water
1 cup yellow cornmeal + extra for dusting
¾ cup all-purpose flour
2 teaspoons baking powder
1 teaspoon salt
1⅓ cups grated sharp cheddar cheese, *divided*
2–3 jalapeño peppers, seeded and finely chopped, *divided*
½ cup creamed corn
¼ cup green scallions, thinly sliced
¾ cup buttermilk
¼ cup butter, melted
¼ cup honey
2 eggs
8 strips cooked bacon, diced

MORNING BREAD

Makes 2 mini loaves

This morning bread recipe is great for any time of the day. You can definitely make this in the oven, but I love how moist and dense it turns out in the Instant Pot. The flavors really come alive, and you can taste the ingredients better.

This is a take on a traditional zucchini bread, but with so much more to offer. The crushed pineapple adds some texture to the bread, and the zucchini helps keep it moist. The only downfall (debatably), just like the Zulu Bread (page 49), is that this is best eaten within 24 hours of making. You can always warm it up in the toaster oven or a few seconds in the microwave to give it some extra life.

Directions

1. In a large bowl, combine sugar and eggs. Mix well. Then add vanilla, oil, zucchini, carrots, crushed pineapple, and currants/raisins.

2. In another bowl, add all dry ingredients and mix well with a whisk. Slowly add dry ingredients to wet ingredients.

3. Lightly spray your mold with nonstick spray. Pour batter into mold. Add 2 cups of warm water to your pot and insert trivet to bottom. Place mold on trivet and lightly cover with foil. Lock lid and close vent. Cook on High Manual Pressure for 40 minutes and NPR (approximately 20–25 minutes).

4. Allow to cool and then serve.

Ingredients

½ cup granulated sugar
2 large eggs
1 teaspoon vanilla extract
1 cup vegetable oil
1 large zucchini, peeled and grated
1 cup carrots, peeled and grated
1 cup crushed pineapple, drained
½ currants or raisins
2 cups all-purpose flour
1 teaspoon ground cinnamon
1 teaspoon baking powder
½ teaspoon baking soda
½ teaspoon sea salt
Nonstick spray
2 cups warm water

You'll Need
7-cup pudding mold
Piece of aluminum foil

CHINESE STEAMED BUNS

Makes 2 dozen

These steamed Chinese buns are insanely delicious and addictive. The recipe is so easy, and the texture is simply fabulous. It's like eating little pillows of air.

If you want to have even more fun with them, you can add in fillings of different meats or sweets to the middle before steaming them (see page 50). However, I love eating them just the way they are. They're perfect little snacks in my book.

Directions

1. Mix together yeast, 1 teaspoon sugar, and ¼ cup warm water. Allow to stand for 30 minutes.

2. Add in ½ cup warm water, flour, salt, 2 tablespoons sugar, baking powder, and vegetable oil. Knead dough until all is smooth and very elastic. Add flour as needed if tacky. Cover and allow to sit for approximately 3 hours. You want your dough to almost triple in size.

3. Once dough is done, punch in the middle. Bring onto a lightly floured surface and knead for a couple of minutes. Then cut the dough in half and roll into 2 long logs. With a pastry knife or blade, cut into 2-inch pieces. You should yield a total of 2 dozen. Place each one on a piece of wax paper.

4. Add 2 cups of water to your pot. Press Sauté and heat until water is almost boiling. Place trivet into pot. Place 5 to 6 pieces of dough into your Instant Pot steamer basket, and place on trivet. Lock lid and close vent. Cook on High Manual Pressure for approximately 16 minutes. When removing lid, remove at an angle as to not drip water on your buns. Remove steamer basket and repeat for remaining buns.

Ingredients

1 tablespoon active dry yeast
2 tablespoons and 1 teaspoon sugar, *divided*
¾ cup warm water, *divided*
1¾ cup all-purpose flour
Pinch of sea salt
2 tablespoons sugar
½ teaspoon baking powder
1 tablespoon vegetable oil
2 cups water

You'll Need

Wax paper cut into 2 x 2-inch squares

Pickled & Fermented

"EASIER THAN I THOUGHT" PICKLES

Makes 2 quarts

I love pickles, but I have an issue: I can't eat them from just any ol' jar. I'm allergic to certain food colorings, and yellow #5 is one of them. Unfortunately, it's used in a lot of pickling spices. I'm not too bothered, though, because I can make my own in my Instant Pot! Yes, it can be done. I used to think making pickles would be a seriously hard process. I was wrong. These pickles stay amazingly crisp and flavorful.

Directions

1. Into a quart-sized sterilized jar, add the cucumber halves and fresh dill.

2. In a small bowl, combine the remaining ingredients. Stir until the sugar and salt have dissolved. Once dissolved, pour into the jar over the cucumbers.

3. Add 1½ cups water to your pot, and place trivet in the bottom. Place lid on jar (finger tight). Lock lid and close vent.

4. Place on High Manual Pressure for 5 minutes. Once done, QPR and remove lid. Allow jar to cool for 5–10 minutes before removing. Allow to cool to room temperature. Place in the fridge for a minimum of 24 hours before enjoying.

Ingredients

1 pound Kirby cucumbers, halved lengthwise and tips cut off

¾ cup fresh dill sprigs

1 cup warm water

½ cup distilled white vinegar

¼ cup sugar

2 tablespoons kosher salt

1 teaspoon whole coriander seeds

1 teaspoon dill seeds

1½ cups water

SAUERKRAUT

Makes approximately 1 quart

Sauerkraut is one of my favorite hot dog toppings. It wasn't until a few years ago that I actually learned how the whole process of making sauerkraut worked. I could've been making my very own this whole time. Sauerkraut is just fermented cabbage. Now do you "need" an Instant Pot to make sauerkraut? No. However, I love using the Yogurt Less Heat function on my pot. The reason is that it keeps everything in a stable temperature environment. Not everybody is lucky enough to have a basement or extra space to store food for fermentation. The Instant Pot is fabulous for fermenting just about anything!

Directions

1. Shred cabbage into thin strips. Sprinkle with sea salt.

2. Add to Instant Pot and knead the cabbage with hands, or pound with a wooden cabbage crusher about 10–12 minutes, until there is enough liquid to cover.

3. Place a weighted trivet or fermentation weight on top of the cabbage to ensure it stays underneath the liquid. If necessary, add a bit of water to completely cover cabbage.

4. Lock lid and close vent. Press Yogurt button with Less Heat. Run cycle for 5 days. Once every 24 hours, QPR any built-up pressure and remove lid to allow air back in.

5. After 5 days, transfer contents from your pot to a jar with a lid. Place in fridge for 2 days for optimal flavor; however, you can start eating it right away!

Ingredients

1 medium head of cabbage
2 tablespoons sea salt

You'll Need

Cabbage crusher or a wooden spoon

KOMBUCHA

Makes 1 gallon

Okay, so I have a confession to make. I don't like kombucha, but I do have several friends that love it. I decided to put my skills to the test to see how it worked out, and it just so happens that it was a hit! It's really hard to go wrong with this recipe, that's how easy it is to make! Many people swear by the health benefits from it, just like they do about drinking apple cider vinegar straight from the bottle. Needless to say, I don't do that, either.

Directions

1. Place tea bags, baking soda, and 6 cups of water into pot. Place on High Manual Pressure for 4 minutes. Once done, let it NPR.

2. Once done, remove the pot from the machine. Remove tea bags and add sugar. Stir well to dissolve.

3. Pour tea into a sanitized glass 1-gallon container. Add remaining 2 cups of water and vinegar or kombucha from a previous batch. Allow to cool completely. It must be cool to the touch.

4. Add your SCOBY. Cover the top of the container with a coffee filter or piece of cheesecloth and lock in place with a rubber band.

5. Place trivet into your Pot and place glass container onto trivet. Add warm water until it reaches the ⅔ max line. Press Yogurt button with Less Heat. Run the Yogurt cycle for 7 days. Keep out of direct sunlight.

6. Decant and enjoy! Place in the fridge in sanitized bottles and caps, or just use it as you go.

Ingredients

3 family-sized black tea bags
¼ teaspoon baking soda
8 cups water, *divided*
1½ cups granulated sugar
1 SCOBY (look for this at Whole Foods or Amazon)
½ cup vinegar or 1 cup Kombucha from a previous batch

EASY PEASY KIMCHI

Makes approximately 2¼ cups

Kimchi is a traditional Korean side dish that is made of salted and fermented vegetables. I love the heat that comes along with the fermented cabbage. If you can be patient, this is a very easy recipe you'll love to make and share.

Directions

1. Place cabbage and radish into your Instant Pot and sprinkle with sea salt. Mix thoroughly with your hands. Press Yogurt Less Heat function. Lock lid and close vent. Allow to sit for 2 hours. QPR any pressure that might have built up. Press Cancel when complete.

2. Thoroughly rinse your cabbage under cold running water. We're trying to remove as much salt as we can. Allow to sit in a colander to drain for at least 20 minutes.

3. Place cabbage back into your Instant Pot. Add all other remaining ingredients and mix well and slowly. We are trying to infuse the flavor of the Korean pepper flakes into your cabbage and radish. Press mixture firmly into pot. Place a steamer basket on top and add a little weight to help keep your mixture a little pressed. I used a round 7-cup Pyrex dish on top of a trivet to keep it weighted down.

4. Press Yogurt button Less Heat. Lock lid and close vent. Allow to sit for 3–4 days. Once every 24 hours, QPR any pressure that might have built up. Remove lid, and firmly press cabbage into liquid. When fermentation is done, place in the fridge to chill and eat when you're ready.

Ingredients

1 head Napa cabbage, cut into quarters or 2-inch wedges, depending on size of cabbage

1 daikon radish peeled and sliced thin

½ cup sea salt

2 tablespoons minced garlic

2 tablespoons minced ginger

1 teaspoon sugar

4 tablespoons Korean red pepper flakes

TOMATILLO "CHOW CHOW"

Makes approximately 2½ cups

Tomatillo "chow chow" is a condiment that you're going to love to have on hand when making Tex-Mex food, or just to add a little pizzazz to any dish you're making. I love how fresh and vibrant the flavor is!

Directions

1. In a blender, add tomatillos, red bell pepper, jalapeño peppers, and onions. Pulse until finely chopped. Transfer to your pot. Stir in salt. Press Yogurt button Less Heat. Allow to sit overnight covered with the lid. You can leave the vent open.

2. Discard any liquid in the pot. You can use a wooden spoon to press liquid out. Add in all remaining ingredients. Press Sauté button. Allow mixture to come to a boil. Stir occasionally. You want the liquid in the pot to evaporate.

3. Transfer to jars with a lid. Allow to cool to room temperature. Transfer to the fridge.

Ingredients

2 pounds chopped tomatillos

1 red bell pepper, deseeded and sliced

2 jalapeño peppers, deseeded and sliced

2 cups Vidalia sweet onions, chopped

½ teaspoon sea salt

1 cup apple cider vinegar

½ cup granulated sugar

½ teaspoon crushed red pepper flakes

¼ teaspoon celery seed

1 tablespoon molasses

PICKLED SPICED CARROTS

Makes 3 pints

I can literally eat these every day and be happy. I love the heat that comes from the peppers and the slight sweetness from the carrots. They play off each other so well. I'm sure this is going to be a fabulous new item that you'll want to make and stock up for your pantry or send around as gifts.

Directions

1. Prepare carrots. Cut off tops and bottoms. You want to cut carrots into thick strips of about 4½ inches in length. I cut mine in half and then in half again.

2. Into a pint-sized sterilized jar, add the carrot strips, a clove of garlic, 8–10 slices of jalapeños, and fresh dill. Repeat this step with another jar to use up all the carrots, garlic, jalapeños, and dill.

3. In a small bowl, combine the white vinegar and pickling salt. Stir until the salt has dissolved. Once dissolved, pour into the jar over the carrot strips.

4. Add 1½ cups water to your pot, and place trivet into the bottom. Place lids on jars (finger tight). Lock lid and close vent.

5. Place on High Manual Pressure for 8 minutes. Once done, QPR and remove lid. Allow jars to cool for 5–10 minutes before removing. Allow to cool to room temperature. Place in the fridge for a minimum of 24 hours before eating.

Ingredients

3 pounds carrots
3 garlic cloves
3–4 jalapeños, sliced thin
7 dill sprigs
3½ cups white vinegar
¼ cup pickling salt
1½ cups water

SANGRIA FRUIT

Makes 3 pints

Sangria is a drink I enjoy all year long. It doesn't have to be summertime for me to enjoy a delicious tall glass of it, or maybe 3. They're so fruity and vibrant, and everyone loves when a small piece of fruit ends up in the glass. Well, why not enjoy just a batch of just sangria fruit? What a great concept! Since it's fruit, it's slightly healthy, right? Of course, you can totally change this from a white wine–based sangria fruit, to a red wine–based one with no problem!

Directions

1. Pour wine into your pot. Press Steam button at Normal setting. Allow wine to boil and be reduced by half. Press the Cancel button and allow to cool. Once cooled, add brandy and Cointreau.

2. Place fruit evenly into 3 pint-sized jars. Evenly distribute wine mixture among jars. Seal lids and allow to cool for 3 hours. Place in the fridge and allow to cool for 48 hours.

Ingredients

1 bottle of Moscato or Riesling
¼ cup brandy
⅓ cup Cointreau
1 kiwi peeled, halved, and sliced
1 orange, unpeeled and sliced thin
1 peach, wedged
1 plum, wedged
15 fresh figs, halved
½ cup red seedless grapes
½ cup green seedless grapes

The Main Bite

GHEE

Makes 1 pint

It's just been the last few months that I learned what ghee actually is, and that I could make it at home in my Instant Pot! I love cooking with ghee, mostly because it has a higher-heat smoking point than traditional butter or olive oil. Ghee is used in many dishes, and something that you're going to love using in your home, too.

Ghee is butter that has the milk solids removed, so it's a class of clarified butter. Plus, you don't have to refrigerate it. You can keep it in a sealed jar right next to the stove.

Directions

1. Place butter into pot and press Sauté button at Normal setting.

2. Once it starts bubbling (approximately 5–6 minutes), adjust to Low Sauté setting. You should see the milk solids separating. In about 18–20 minutes, you will see that the milk solids have turned to a light golden-brown color. You have to pay attention or you will burn it. You want the milk solids to have a beautiful brown color. That's how you know it's done.

3. Once you achieve the color, remove the metal pot so it doesn't continue to cook and burn. Press the Cancel button to stop the heat.

4. Allow to cool for a couple of minutes. Strain melted butter through cheesecloth. Allow to cool and set. Your ghee is done!

Ingredients

1 pound grass-fed unsalted butter

EASY MORNING FRITTATA

Serves 6–8

If you plan on hosting a brunch, or want to make a quick and delicious breakfast, then this frittata is the perfect choice for you. Even if you're running late, you can easily multitask this recipe. It's versatile, so you can add whatever veggies you would like.

Directions

1. Put trivet in the bottom of the pot and add 1 cup of water.

2. In a bowl, whisk eggs, milk, flour, salt, and pepper. Add veggies and 1 cup of cheese until combined.

3. Pour the mixture into a 7-inch cake pan or other dish that will fit, lightly coated with nonstock spray. Cover the top with foil and place on top of the trivet.

4. Lock the lid and close the vent. Cook for 30 minutes on High Manual Pressure.

5. Once done, allow to NPR for 10 minutes. QPR the remaining pressure.

6. Remove frittata from pot, and sprinkle the top with the remaining cheese. Place foil back on top to help melt the cheese.

Ingredients

1 cup water
8 large eggs
½ cup milk
½ cup flour
Sea salt and cracked pepper to taste
1 large red pepper, diced into small cubes
1 cup tomatoes, sliced or chopped
½ cup baby kale, sliced thin
1½ cups shredded Colby Jack cheese

SWEDISH MEATBALLS

Serves 6

I need to make this dish more often. It's easy to make, and it doesn't cause me a lot of stress to make for the family. I cook the pasta separately while the meatballs are cooking in the Instant Pot. I don't cook them with the meatballs because of the different cooking times of the pasta. My family loved it, so it looks like I'll be making this in the near future.

Directions

1. In a bowl add all ingredients for the meatballs. Mix well with a wooden spoon or your hands. Form meatballs and set them on parchment paper. Make them the size of 50-cent pieces.

2. Turn on the pot's Sauté setting, and add olive oil. Once heated, add about 12–15 meatballs. You are going to sear on all sides until lightly browned. Remove meatballs and set to the side once done. You will have to work your meatballs in batches.

3. Add beef broth and stir to deglaze the pan. Add butter, Dijon mustard, Worcestershire sauce, and 1 cup of the heavy cream (reserve the remaining 1 cup). Stir well. Press the Cancel button.

4. Add the meatballs back into the pot. Lock the lid and close the vent.

5. Cook on High Manual Pressure for 6 minutes. Let it NPR for 10 minutes. QPR remaining pressure.

6. Whisk remaining heavy cream with flour and cornstarch until there are no lumps. Remove meatballs and set to the side. Press Sauté in Normal mode and mix in the flour/cream mixture. Bring to a simmer, stirring frequently, until thickened. Once thickened, press Cancel. Add meatballs back in and give a gentle stir.

Meatballs Ingredients

1½ lb. ground beef (90% lean)
½ cup panko bread crumbs
½ cup milk
1 medium Vidalia sweet onion, diced fine
1 teaspoon sea salt
½ teaspoon cracked pepper
¼ teaspoon allspice
¼ teaspoon nutmeg
1 teaspoon garlic powder
1 egg, beaten

Sauce Ingredients

2 tablespoons olive oil
2½ cups beef broth
6 tablespoons salted butter, *divided*
1 teaspoon Dijon mustard
1 teaspoon Worcestershire sauce
2 cups heavy cream, *divided*
¼ cup flour
1 tablespoon cornstarch

CITRUS-MARINATED TILAPIA

Serves 4

I love meal prepping because it makes my life so much easier, and this is one that you can prep in advance and have ready for dinner. Plus it's one of my favorite types of dishes: the kind that are easy to clean up afterward.

We are using a slightly unconventional sous vide method with cooking the fish in FoodSaver/sous vide bags. The fish will turn out heavenly. I served it over a bed of kale and couscous. However, you can certainly serve it over a bed of rice or pasta.

Directions

1. In a bowl, mix olive oil, lemon juice, lime juice, salt, and pepper. Mix well.

2. Sprinkle each piece of tilapia with a little salt and pepper. Place each one in a bag. Place 1 tablespoon of the citrus liquid we made into each bag.

3. Top each piece of tilapia with a slice of lemon and lime. Seal each bag—not too tight or liquid will pour out.

4. Add 3 cups warm water to your pot. Place trivet at the bottom. Then add the 4 bags of sealed tilapia into the water. Lock lid and close vent. Put on High Manual Pressure for 5 minutes. Allow to NPR for 5 minutes and then QPR the remaining pressure. Remove bags and allow to cool for a couple of minutes before cutting open and serving.

Ingredients

2 tablespoons extra-virgin olive oil

Juice of 1 lemon

Juice of 1 lime

Sea salt and cracked pepper to taste

4 pieces tilapia

4 FoodSaver bags that have been portioned off for the size of the tilapia plus a little extra space.

1 lemon, sliced into thin wheels

1 lime, sliced into thin wheels

3 cups warm water

INSTANT POT MAGIC

ZULU BREAD IN CHICKEN HARISSA BROTH

Serves 6

Zulu bread is a traditional South African steamed bread. When Zulu bread is made, it is meant to be consumed that day. The bread is traditionally steamed in a plastic bag, and is often paired with a tomato-based soup. Most steamed breads do not have a long shelf life. They wind up being extra dry and sort of dense.

This dish is just fabulous. I love spicy food, so it was perfect for me. If you love heat, add in another tablespoon of harissa paste. It will be spicy, but you'll find that you can't stop eating it. The Zulu bread helps to absorb some of the heat.

Directions

1. In a bowl, combine yeast, sugar, and water. Wait 5–6 minutes, or until yeast starts to have bubbles. Once bubbles have formed, add in salt, flour, and cornmeal. Mix well until you have a soft ball.

2. Knead dough in bowl until you have a pliable dough; add more water if necessary. Knead for about 10 minutes, or until soft and elastic. Place in a lightly oiled bowl and leave in a warm place to rise for about an hour.

3. Punch the dough and knead for 2–3 more minutes. Roll into a round ball of dough. Allow the dough to rise for 5 minutes.

4. While waiting for dough to rise, make harissa broth. Turn pot on to Sauté Normal mode. Add olive oil and wait until heated. Once heated, add chicken sausage. Cook until sausage has a slight sear on it.

5. Add in remaining ingredients. Bring to a slight boil. Once boiling has begun, add your Zulu dough to the center. Cook on High Manual Pressure for 20 minutes and allow to NPR for 10 minutes. QPR any remaining pressure.

6. Remove lid and allow mixture to cool for a minute or two. With a spatula, remove the Zulu bread from the broth and place on cutting board. Serve slices of the bread with the soup.

Dough Ingredients

1 teaspoon instant dry yeast
4 teaspoons granulated sugar
1 cup warm water
½ teaspoon salt
1 cup all-purpose flour
1 cup cornmeal

Broth Ingredients

2 tablespoons olive oil
12 oz. chicken sausage, sliced
1 teaspoon sea salt
1 tablespoon harissa paste
4 cups chicken stock
Sea salt and cracked pepper, to taste

HAWAIIAN STEAMED BEEF BUNS

Makes 8

Hawaiian steamed beef buns are like little pillows of beefy heaven. It's a brand-new way to use ground beef for most people, and a fabulous dough to use. This recipe is totally foolproof, even when making the dough.

In this recipe, we are going to use the Steam function. It's a cooking function that is not utilized enough on the Instant Pot. This overlooked function can do so much!

Dough

1. Whisk together warm water and honey in a small bowl. Sprinkle in the yeast. Let the mixture rest until it bubbles, 4–6 minutes.

2. Whisk together the flour and salt in a large bowl. Add the yeast mixture and olive oil. Stir with a wooden spoon until just combined. If the dough seems dry, sprinkle in a little bit of water. Turn the dough out onto a clean work surface. If the dough is sticky, lightly dust the surface with flour. Knead the dough until it is smooth and elastic. This will take about 5–10 minutes.

3. Lightly grease a large mixing bowl with a nonstick spray. Form the dough into a ball and place it in the bowl, gently turning to coat. Cover with a damp clean cloth and let rest in a warm place until doubled in size, approximately 1 hour.

Filling

1. Turn pot on in Sauté mode and add canola oil. Once heated, add onion. Cook onion until softened. Add ground beef, salt, pepper, and garlic. Cook until all pink coloration is gone from the beef.

2. Add in all remaining ingredients. Stir thoroughly. Cook mixture until sauce has thickened. Once done, press the Cancel button. Allow mixture to completely cool.

Dough Ingredients

¾ cup warm water
3 tablespoons honey
¼-ounce package active dry yeast
3 cups all-purpose flour, plus more
    for dusting if necessary
½ teaspoon sea salt
2 teaspoons olive oil

You'll Need

8 (3-inch) squares of wax paper

Filling Ingredients

2 teaspoons canola oil, plus more
    for greasing
1 medium Vidalia sweet onion, diced
½ pound ground beef
Sea salt and cracked pepper to
    taste
2 cloves garlic, minced
¾ teaspoon Chinese five-spice
    blend
¼ cup warm water
2 tablespoons soy sauce
2 tablespoons hoisin sauce

Assembly

1. Punch dough and divide into 8 equal-sized portions.
2. Flatten a piece of dough and place about 2 tablespoons of filling in the middle. Pinch the edges and seal the bun. Place sealed edges onto wax paper. Place a damp cloth over buns and allow 45 minutes to rise.
3. Add 2 cups of warm water to pot and place trivet at bottom. Press Steam and allow water to get hot.
4. Place 3 buns (including wax paper) onto an Instant Pot silicone steamer basket. You want at least a ½–1 inch of space in between the buns. Place on trivet and place glass lid on top. Cook for approximately 12–15 minutes. Remove lid at an angle. Replenish water as needed.

CHILI LIME STEAK AND AVOCADO BOWL

Serves 4–5

This is an easy and healthy meal to make for your family at any given time. The most work you have to put in is cutting up the avocado when it's time to serve. You can always add a side of steamed veggies and serve over a bed of rice.

I live for easy and delicious meals to make for the family. This is a great freezer meal prep item. Minus the avocados, you can place all of the ingredients into a freezer-safe container for later use.

Directions

1. Turn your IP on Sauté and add olive oil. Once hot, add garlic and cook until a golden color. Then add all remaining ingredients (except avocados), and mix well with wooden spoon.

2. Lock lid, close vent, and cook on Manual High Pressure for 10 minutes.

3. After 10 minutes, do a QPR. Once pressure is released, press Cancel and remove lid.

4. Press Sauté button, and stir the meat to break it up into little chunks.

5. Keep on Sauté mode until liquid has been reduced by half.

6. Allow to cool and serve in a bowl. Surround the meat with your diced avocado.

Ingredients

1 tablespoon extra-virgin olive oil

1 teaspoon minced garlic

1½–2 pounds of fajita steak strips or skirt steak (cut into cubes)

1 tablespoon water

2 teaspoons lime juice

½ teaspoon chili powder

½ teaspoon sea salt

½ teaspoon cracked pepper

1 teaspoon Cholula, or your favorite hot sauce

2–3 diced avocados

ZESTY PINEAPPLE CHICKEN

Serves 5

I don't have a lot of one-pot dump recipes on hand, but this is my easy go-to that I use for my family a lot, and I see clean plates every single time. It's perfect to eat by itself or served over rice. If you like a little more spice in your life, then don't be afraid to add in extra Cajun seasoning to the pot.

Directions

1. Place all ingredients into the pot liner of your Instant Pot. Lock the lid and close the vent. Place on High Manual Pressure for 12 minutes, and allow to NPR.

2. Once depressurized, open the vent to ensure that all pressure has been released. Pull out the chicken breasts onto a plate or cutting board, and shred with forks. Once the chicken is shredded, add it back into your IP. Let it set for a couple of minutes to marinate in the pineapple juice base before serving.

Ingredients

3 pounds boneless skinless chicken breast

12 oz. jar Trader Joe's Pineapple Salsa

40 oz. Dole Tropical Gold Pineapple chunks (including the juice from the cans)

¼ teaspoon Slap Ya Mama (or other Cajun seasoning)

1 teaspoons sea salt

GHORMEH SABZI

Serves 4

This is a traditional and popular Persian dish with very strong roots in Iran. It's vibrant, fresh, and full of flavors. Its literal translation is "herb stew," as it's made with lots of fresh herbs. The two standout ingredients you might not have heard of or used before are fenugreek and limoo amami (black limes). Those two ingredients are key to making the flavor profile. Fenugreek really gives it a special flavor, as it almost has a maple syrup flavor to it. So, if you're not able to purchase it online or in a store, you can substitute a tablespoon of maple syrup in place of it.

Directions

1. Turn your Instant Pot on Sauté mode. Add butter and yellow onion. Cook for approximately 2 minutes.

2. Add your meat, and then all remaining ingredients. Just be sure that the meat is on the bottom. I added the kidney beans last on top of the all of the ingredients.

3. Lock your lid and close the vent. Place on High Manual Pressure for 15 minutes, then let it NPR for about 18 to 20 minutes.

4. Once done, release any remaining pressure. Remove lid at an angle to ensure you're not dripping on yourself by accident. Give it a good stir before serving.

Ingredients

1 tablespoon salted butter

1 large yellow onion, finely chopped

1½ lb. lamb or beef stew meat, cubed

4 bunches parsley (leaves only)

1 bunch cilantro (leaves only)

4 leeks, diced

1 tablespoon dried fenugreek (or 1 bunch fresh fenugreek)

4 dried black limes (*limoo amani*), or 4 tablespoons lemon juice (if *limoo mani* is unavailable)

1 tablespoon turmeric

Sea salt

Cracked black pepper

1 cup water (I used hot water to help build pressure faster)

1 cup dark red kidney beans, drained

Apps, Soups, and Sides

CHEESY POTATOES AU GRATIN

Serves 6

This is such a quick and easy side dish to make your family or your next potluck event. It hits all the right notes of creamy, cheesy, and lots of delicious potatoes.

This is one of the recipes I mentioned where we use the Instant Pot to cook everything, but then we finish it in the oven.

Now, can you use potatoes other than russets? You can, but the texture is going to be so different, as each type of potato has different starch cells. So, some potatoes might give you that icky, pasty kind of taste. Stick with russets, and you'll be happy.

Directions

1. Place potatoes and chicken broth into your pot. Place on High Manual Pressure for 1 minute.

2. Press Cancel. Carefully remove the potatoes and place in them in a greased baking dish.

3. To the remaining chicken broth in your pot, add in all remaining ingredients, except ½ cup reserved cheese. Press Sauté button in Normal mode. Preheat your oven on broil.

4. Stir until you have achieved a creamy and velvety texture, approximately 2–3 minutes. Press Cancel. Pour your sauce over the potatoes and then cover with remaining ½ cup cheese.

5. Place baking dish under broiler in oven for approximately 2 minutes, or until you have a beautiful golden-brown crust on top. Allow to cool and serve.

Ingredients

7 russet potatoes, skin on and sliced ¼-inch thick

1 cup chicken broth

4 oz. cream cheese, room temperature

2 tablespoons heavy cream

1 cup milk

1½ + ½ (reserved) cup sharp cheddar shredded cheese, fresh grated

½ cup grated Parmesan cheese

2 garlic cloves, minced

Sea salt and cracked pepper to taste

VEGETABLE DETOX SOUP

Serves 8

Sometimes our bodies need a little recharge of nutrients to help detox. This is a classic recipe—now, this recipe is going to scare you when you start putting it together. Your pot is going to be crammed full of ingredients that are great for your body.

This is such a hearty soup! If you wish to add more liquid, you can do so in the end when adding your baby spinach.

Directions

1. Add all ingredients to your pot, except baby spinach and green onions. Lock lid and close vent. Cook for 6 minutes on High Manual Pressure. As you add in your kale, don't be afraid to push those ingredients down into the pot. Once your ingredients start cooking away, the kale and cabbage are going to release moisture and wilt. Just try to leave a divot around where the pressure pin is.

2. Once done, QPR any pressure. Remove lid, and add baby spinach and green onions. Stir until spinach has wilted into your soup. Serve away! Stores great in the freezer.

Ingredients

4 large carrots, peeled and sliced
½ head of cabbage (for convenience, you can use 2 cups pre-shredded coleslaw mix)
2 Vidalia sweet onions, diced
1 head of garlic, peeled and chopped
2 cups fresh or frozen green beans, cut into bite size pieces
10 ounces of fresh kale, tough stems removed and chopped
6 cups vegetable broth
12 ounces salsa
1 tablespoon chili powder
2 teaspoons dried oregano
2 teaspoons cumin
2 teaspoons paprika
Salt and pepper to taste
7 green onions, sliced
6 ounces fresh baby spinach leaves

GAME DAY PIZZA DIP

Serves 8

Everyone loves making appetizers for the big games once the weekend gets here. My fabulous friend, Melissa, gave me this simple recipe that I used to make in the oven all the time. Until one day that it dawned on me that I can make it just as easily in my Instant Pot without having to heat up my whole kitchen. Now, I can make it any time of the year!

Directions

1. You need a 7-cup Pyrex dish (or other oven-safe dish). Make sure that your cream cheese has come to room temperature to make sure it's pliable. Place the block of cream cheese into bottom of the dish and spread out as evenly as you can with the back of a spoon.

2. Add your layer of sauce, and spread around evenly. Sprinkle your mozzarella cheese around to create an even coating, then sprinkle the basil on top. You don't have to add basil, but I love the freshness it adds.

3. Add 2 cups of water into your pot, and place the trivet inside of your liner. Please make sure the liner is inside of your IP before you pour your water into it!

4. Place the Pyrex dish full of pizza dip ingredients into your IP on top of your trivet. Lock the lid and close the vent. Place on High Manual Pressure for 20 minutes.

5. Once done, do a quick release. Remove lid at angle so that the moisture droplets from the lid doesn't pour into your pizza dip.

6. Allow the trivet handles to cool for a minute or two before removing from your machine.

Ingredients

8 oz. cream cheese, room temperature

½ cup spaghetti sauce or pizza sauce (I used basil flavored)

1 cup shredded mozzarella cheese

½ teaspoon chopped basil

2 cups water

DEVILED EGGS SQUARED

Makes 12

Who doesn't love deviled eggs, especially when you can make them so much more easily by not having to peel the eggshells off the eggs? I love the fact that they're easy to eat when they're in a square shape; that alone jazzes up the appearance.

Directions

1. Crack and separate the yolks from the whites into two mixing bowls. Set aside the yolks. Whip the whites just until frothy. Pour into dish, and then cover with foil.

2. Whip egg yolks until blended, and set to the side.

3. Pour 1½ cups of water into your pot and place trivet into bottom. Place in your dish of egg whites, lock the lid and close the vent. Put on High Manual Pressure for 6 minutes. NPR for 2 minutes, and then QPR the rest of the pressure.

4. Remove dish from the pot and allow to cool to room temperature. Once cooled, place in the fridge for 15–20 minutes. Drain water from your Instant Pot.

5. Turn machine on in Sauté mode and lightly spray bottom of inner pot with nonstick spray. Once hot, add yolks. You will want to constantly stir the egg yolks so you don't overcook them by accident—it's not fun having to start all over again.

6. Take out cooked egg yolks, and flake with a fork. Then add mayonnaise, mustard, salt, and pepper. Mix well with a fork. Place contents into a pastry bag. Place in fridge to cool for about 10–12 minutes.

7. Retrieve the egg whites from the fridge. Remove egg whites from the dish and place on a cutting board. With a sharp knife, cut 2 equally spaced lines vertically, and then 4 equally spaced lines horizontally. You will wind up with 12 pieces.

8. With the pastry bag, create dollops of yolk mixture on top of each piece. Garnish with paprika and pieces of scallions. Place back in the fridge until ready to serve.

Ingredients

8 large eggs
1½ cups water
¼ cup mayonnaise
2 tablespoons yellow mustard
Sea salt and freshly ground black pepper (to taste)
Paprika to garnish
Scallions, to garnish

You'll Need

1 – Three-cup Pyrex dish (7x5)
A piece of aluminum foil

MISO SOUP

Serves 4

Miso soup is just fabulous anytime. It's a perfect hearty soup. I love mushrooms, so this soup is right up my alley. I no longer have to wait to go to my one of my favorite restaurants to grab a bowl of miso soup, I can now make it at home.

It just doesn't get any easier than this.

Directions

1. Press Sauté button at Normal setting. Once pot is hot, add olive oil, garlic, ginger, and mushrooms. Cook for 5–7 minutes, being sure to stir occasionally.

2. Press Cancel and allow pot to cool for 5 minutes.

3. Add all remaining ingredients to pot except the tofu. Press High Manual Pressure and cook for 5 minutes. Once done, QPR all pressure. Remove lid, and add in tofu. The tofu will heat up in no time, and then it's ready to serve!

Ingredients

3 tablespoons olive oil

1 teaspoon minced garlic

1 tablespoon ginger, peeled and minced

4 ounces shiitake or maitake mushrooms, sliced thin

Sea salt and pepper, to taste

1 cup chopped kale

4 cups miso broth

½ teaspoon chili flakes

1 pack extra-firm tofu, cut into 1-inch cubes

COLLARD GREENS WITH HAM HOCKS

Serves 6

I can eat collard greens all day long! The smokiness of the ham hocks adds so much dimension to the greens. The biggest rule when making greens is to make sure you wash, wash, and wash them some more. Unless you take the shortcut and buy a bag of chopped collard greens, you have to make sure that all of the sand and grit is out of the greens. There's nothing worse than gritty greens.

Everyone has their own favorite ingredients and levels of spice when they make their greens. If you want to spice it up, add more hot sauce or some red pepper flakes.

Directions

1. Add all ingredients into your pot, layering ham hocks on top of greens. Set on High Manual Pressure for 16 minutes and QPR all pressure.

2. Remove ham hocks from pot and pull meat off the bone and add back to the pot before serving. Make the Jalapeño Bacon Corn Bread (page 17) to enjoy with it!

Ingredients

2 bunches collard greens (triple washed and veins removed), rough chopped

1 cup chicken broth

1 cup water

2 ham hocks

1 tablespoon garlic, minced

2 tablespoons Cholula hot sauce (or your favorite)

2 tablespoons apple cider vinegar

Sea salt and cracked pepper to taste

STEWED TOMATOES

Makes approximately 4 cups

In the South, stewed tomatoes can be found in every household, just like sweet tea. Everyone jazzes their stewed tomatoes up a little differently with spices, and some put in okra and corn. No matter how you make it, it's always best served over rice or with a nice buttered biscuit.

Directions

1. Place all ingredients into your pot. Lock lid and close vent. Cook on High Manual Pressure for 12 minutes. Once done, QPR the pressure. It's ready to serve!

Ingredients

4½ cups tomatoes, peeled and diced
1 bell pepper, diced
1 small Vidalia sweet onion, diced
¼ teaspoon hot pepper flakes
1 teaspoon garlic, minced
½ cup water

SMASHIN' MASHED CARROTS

Serves 4

This is going to be one of your favorite new sides to make with any dish. It's quick, easy, and delicious. I use baby carrots because they tend to carry a little bit more sweetness, though they're basically chopped-up carrots. They also purée well with the immersion blender. Quick tip: Be sure to place a towel around the immersion blender to avoid splatters.

Directions

1. Add baby carrots and water to pot. Lock lid and close vent. Cook on High Manual Pressure for 4 minutes. QPR any pressure.

2. Drain water from pot. Add in all remaining ingredients. Use an immersion blender to "mash" your carrots until you get a creamy and velvety texture.

Ingredients

2 pounds baby carrots
1 cup water
2 tablespoons salted butter
2 tablespoons Greek yogurt
1 tablespoon honey
1 tablespoon light brown sugar

Immersion blender is required for this recipe

HASH BROWN CASSEROLE "FUNERAL POTATOES"

Serves 6

Yes. Funeral potatoes—the name has been around for a while. These are so delicious and comforting, which is why it's traditionally been made for friends and family members that experienced a passing (but feel free to enjoy it anytime!).

This is definitely one great big bowl of comfort food right here.

Directions

1. Press Sauté and add unsalted butter.

2. Add the onion and cook it until soft. Add the garlic and Sauté for 30–45 seconds.

3. Press Cancel. Add the salt, pepper, and red pepper flakes.

4. Pour in the chicken broth and deglaze the bottom of the pan.

5. Place steamer basket into the pot and pour in frozen hash browns.

6. Lock lid and close the vent. Cook on High Manual Pressure for 2 minutes. Once done, do a QPR.

7. Remove the hash browns from steamer basket, combine with sour cream and cheese, and stir everything together.

8. Transfer potatoes to an 8-inch greased baking or casserole dish and set it aside.

9. Preheat oven to 400°F. In a medium bowl, add 2 tablespoons melted butter and panko bread crumbs. Mix well with a fork until mixture is well combined. Scatter breadcrumb mixture across top of potatoes. Place in the oven for approximately 10–12 minutes, or until crumb topping is golden brown.

Ingredients

2 tablespoons unsalted butter +
    2 tablespoons, melted
1 small white onion, chopped
4 cloves garlic, minced
½ teaspoon salt
¼ teaspoon black pepper
⅛ teaspoon crushed red pepper
    flakes
1 cup chicken broth
26 ounces hash browns (1 large
    bag, shredded, frozen)
2 cups shredded cheddar cheese
¾ cup sour cream
1 cup bread crumbs (panko)

CAJUN SPICED BOILED PEANUTS

Makes 1 pound

I might still be showing my southern roots with this little delicacy. Boiled peanuts are everywhere you go down South. Go to the nearest gas station, and you'll find a big pot of boiled peanuts simmering away. Drive down a dirt road, and you'll see a boiled peanuts stand right next to a fruitcake stand. I am not kidding about either.

Directions

1. Place all ingredients into your Instant Pot and stir with a wooden spoon to mix the ingredients around in the pot.

2. Close lid, and set your IP on High Manual Pressure for 30 minutes, and then let it NPR.

3. Make sure all steam is released, remove lid, and serve! I like mine warm and not too hot.

Recipe Notes

Please note that this cooking time will result in slightly firm peanuts. I don't like my boiled peanuts too soft. If you want southern style "Slurpee" peanuts, then add an additional 45–50 minutes on the manual timer and allow to NPR.

Ingredients

1 pound raw peanuts in the shell
¼ cup sea salt
1 teaspoon white distilled vinegar
7 cups water
1 tablespoon Slap Ya Mama (or other Cajun seasoning)

BEEF POT STICKERS

Makes 48

You no longer have to order takeout to enjoy pot stickers any day of the week. They're easy to assemble, once you get the hang of it. When I first started making pot stickers, I had issues with sealing the edges. I used too little water, and I couldn't get them to close. By the time I was done, I was a pot sticker-making pro.

I love that you can make any type of filling to put inside them: beef, pork, vegetables, seafood, chicken, whatever you're in the mood for.

Directions

1. In a large bowl, combine all ingredients except the beef and wrappers. Add beef; mix lightly and thoroughly. Place a teaspoon of filling in the center of each wrapper. Moisten wrapper edges with water. Fold wrapper over filling; seal edges to form a pleated pouch. Stand pot stickers on your work surface to flatten bottoms. Keep dumplings covered with a moist cloth until ready to cook.

2. Place 2 cups of water and trivet into your pot, press Steam and allow water to boil. Place dumplings in a steamer basket. Place basket on trivet. Place your Instant Pot glass lid on top and cook for approximately 5–6 minutes or until cooked through.

Ingredients

4 green onions, thinly sliced

2 tablespoons reduced-sodium soy sauce

2 garlic cloves, minced

1 tablespoon rice vinegar

1 tablespoon minced fresh ginger root

¼ teaspoon coarsely ground pepper

1 pound ground beef

48 pot sticker or gyoza wrappers

2 cups water

QUICK *SOUPE DE POISSON*

Serves 4

This is a classic Mediterranean recipe, the French translation is "fish soup." It's rich in texture, has loads of flavor, and the color is beautiful to look at. Most garnish the soup with thick chunks of bread that each have a smear of mayonnaise on top of it.

The making of soupe de poisson *is a collective endeavor. In the coastal Mediterranean cities, the whole family is normally involved, from catching the fresh seafood to preparing it in the kitchen.*

I call this a *"quick"* soupe de poisson *because I use lobster bisque and fish stock in it. Normally, you're simmering shrimp shells and fish carcasses for hours to make an amazing stock. I cheated because I don't have that type of time. My family gets hungry pretty fast.*

Directions

1. Turn your pot on in Normal Sauté mode and add oil. Once oil is heated, add onions, and cook, stirring often, until they start to soften.

2. Add seafood, tomatoes, garlic, and fennel, then stir for 2 minutes. Add bay leaves, orange rind, thyme, and tomato paste and stir to combine. Add the fish stock. Bring to a slight boil.

3. Once brought to a boil, press the Cancel button. Wait 5 minutes, and then lock the lid and close the vent. Cook on High Manual Pressure for 10 minutes and allow to NPR. Strain contents through a sieve, pressing down on solids to extract all the flavor that you can.

4. Press Sauté button in Less Heat setting. Return stock to your pot and add lobster bisque and simmer. Cook for 10–15 minutes until slightly reduced. Stir in cream, then simmer for 1 minute until heated through.

Ingredients

2 tablespoons olive oil

2 Vidalia sweet onions, roughly chopped

2 pounds mixed seafood (salmon, white fish, and whole prawns work best)

5 tomatoes, chopped

2 garlic cloves, minced

1 fennel bulb, chopped

2 bay leaves

1 long strip pared orange rind

3 sprigs of thyme

1 tablespoon tomato paste

4 cups fish stock

2 cups lobster bisque

½ cup heavy cream

STEAMED CLAMS WITH BACON AND FRIED BREAD

Serves 2

These clams are so succulent. The house fills with a great aroma, and everyone comes out of the darkest depths of the house to follow their nose to your Instant Pot. The bacon alone is enough to get the people in the house going, and everything else is just adds to the excitement.

This is one of those perfect recipes to make on a lovely day that has a slight chill in the air. You can open a bottle of your favorite bottle of wine to enjoy with it.

Directions

1. Press Sauté on pot. Add olive oil and allow to heat. Once heated, add bread. Stir until evenly coated and slightly crisped.

2. Remove bread and then add bacon pieces. Cook bacon until slightly crisp. Remove bacon from the pot, leaving the bacon grease.

3. To the bacon grease, add onion and garlic. Sauté until onion is translucent.

4. Add in pepper flakes, oregano, herbes de Provence, salt, pepper, and tomato paste. Stir until well mixed. Then add in white wine. Mix thoroughly.

5. Add in 2 cups of warm water. Bring to a boil— maintain boil for about 10 minutes.

6. Add in cooked bacon and clams. Once clams have been added, place lid on top (you can leave vent open). Cook for approximately 6 minutes. Stir clams occasionally until all are fully opened.

7. To make serving easier, remove clams into a separate bowl so you can serve. Place clams into bowl, add about ¼ of the crisp bread croutons, and ladle the broth over the clams. For a fresh, vibrant color, you can add chopped parsley on top.

Ingredients

½ cup olive oil

2 cups rustic bread

6 slices thick-cut bacon, cut into 1-inch pieces

1 medium Vidalia sweet onion, diced

1½ tablespoons garlic, minced

¼ teaspoon red pepper flakes

¼ teaspoon dried oregano

1 teaspoon herbes de Provence

Sea salt and fresh cracked pepper

2 tablespoons tomato paste

1 cup dry white wine

2 cups warm water

32 littleneck clams, scrubbed

Sweet Treats

MINI PINEAPPLE UPSIDE-DOWN CAKES

Makes 8

This is one of the most classic desserts that you can make in your Instant Pot. I decided to make these in a mini version so everyone could have their own individual cake. Not too many of the mouths in my family are willing to share. If you don't happen to have little molds or ramekins to make them in, you can always use silicone cupcake molds!

Directions

1. In a large bowl, mix together the flour, baking powder, salt, melted butter, sugar, eggs, and vanilla until smooth.

2. Spray each ramekin with a light coating of nonstick spray.

3. Add a slice of butter to each ramekin, then sprinkle about 1 teaspoon of brown sugar into bottom of each ramekin, spreading evenly. Then add a cherry in the middle and 1½ tablespoons crushed pineapple around it.

4. Evenly distribute batter to ramekins, on top of the pineapple.

5. Add 1½ cups water to your pot and place trivet in the bottom of the pot. Place ramekins in a pyramid formation onto the trivet—three on the bottom (spaced out), and one in the middle on top of the rims of the other three.

6. Lock the lid and close your vent. Cook on High Manual Pressure for 9 minutes. Once done, QPR the pressure. Allow a few minutes to cool, and carefully remove the ramekins with tongs.

7. While the first batch is cooling, add your second batch to the Instant Pot. When ready to serve, simply turn onto your plate, upside down.

Ingredients

2 cups flour
1 tablespoon baking powder
1 teaspoon salt
½ cup butter, melted + ½ cup cold, cut into 8 slices
1½ cups sugar
2 eggs
1 teaspoon vanilla
½ cup brown sugar
8 maraschino cherries
1 can crushed pineapple, drained
Nonstick spray

You'll Need

8 (4-ounce) ramekins

PEA PICKER'S CAKE

Makes 8 mini cakes

This is hands down one of my favorite desserts. I love everything about it. Everything from the pineapple cake to the chilled mandarin orange segments on top, I love it all. I first came across this cake at the weekly church dinner—once I took a bite, it was pure heaven. I never tasted anything like it before, and now I will never have to worry because I have the recipe to make it whenever I want to. It's like the cake version of an ambrosia salad.

Directions

1. In one bowl, combine the topping ingredients together. Cover and place in the fridge.

2. In a large bowl, mix together the flour, baking powder, salt, melted butter, sugar, eggs, and vanilla until smooth.

3. Remove 8 mandarin segments and set to the side. Add the remaining mandarin oranges plus the juice into the batter. Mix well.

4. Lightly coat the ramekins with the nonstick spray. Evenly distribute batter to ramekins.

5. Place 1 cup of water in your pot and place trivet at the bottom of the pot. Place ramekins in a pyramid formation onto the trivet—three on the bottom (spaced out), and one in the middle on top of the rims of the other three.

6. Lock lid and close vent. Cook on High Manual Pressure for 9 minutes, and then QPR once done.

7. Remove and allow to cool on a baker's rack. While cooling, work on your second batch. Allow ramekins to cool for 10 minutes, and then place in the fridge for 1 hour.

8. Remove cakes from ramekins. Cover with topping and garnish with a mandarin orange segment.

Topping Ingredients

16 ounces Cool Whip topping
20 ounce can pineapple, crushed and drained, reserving the juice
3 ounce box instant vanilla pudding

Cake Ingredients

2 cups flour
1 tablespoon baking powder
1 teaspoon salt
½ cup melted butter
1½ cups sugar
2 eggs
1 teaspoon vanilla extract
15 ounce can mandarin orange segments (Do not drain! You will use the juice in the cake mix.)
Nonstick spray

You'll Need

8 (4 ounce) ramekins

CHOCOLATE TOFU SURPRISE

Makes 1 tart, or 12 minis

This superrich chocolate cake is going to surprise you! This recipe comes from one of my greatest friends, executive chef Bobby Trigg. I was bouncing ideas off him, and he said that I'd totally be able to utilize the Instant Pot for this. He was so right!

The one thing to remember about tofu is that it is completely tasteless. It absorbs flavors that it's prepared with in recipes. The couscous just adds the right amount of crunch and texture that's needed to help balance this dessert. I give the directions on how to make it in a pie shell, but I love having fun with food—so I made mine in mini molds. Let your imagination go crazy with the different molds that you can use the recipe for.

If you're a vegan, then you are in luck! This is a 100 percent vegan dessert, just make sure you're using the right chocolate chips.

Crust Directions

1. To your pot, add water, chocolate chips, sugar, cocoa, and vanilla extract. Press Sauté and bring ingredients to a simmer. During the process, stir until the chocolate chips have melted and it has started to thicken a little.

2. Once the thickening process has started, press the Cancel button on your pot. Stir in the couscous. Let it rest in the mixture for 2–3 minutes, and then remove the pot from the machine. Allow to cool for 15–20 minutes. Spread the crust evenly into the bottom of a 9-inch springform pan. Clean and dry your pot for next portion of recipe.

Filling Directions

1. Press Sauté button at Low Heat setting on your machine. Add sugar, chocolate chips, and 1 tablespoon of water (add extra water as needed). Stir constantly to ensure that you get a smooth mixture.

2. Once you've achieved the smooth mixture, remove pot from machine. To a blender or food processor, add chocolate mixture, tofu, and cocoa powder. Blend until completely smooth. Pour your tofu filling into the crust-lined pan. Cover and place in the fridge for at least 2 hours before serving. Overnight works best.

Crust Ingredients

1¼ cups water

1½ cups semisweet chocolate chips

6 tablespoons granulated sugar

6 tablespoons unsweetened cocoa

1 tablespoon vanilla extract

¾ cup couscous

Tofu Filling Ingredients

½ cup sugar

2 cups semisweet chocolate chips

2 tablespoons water, as needed

19 ounces silken tofu, drained well

½ cup unsweetened cocoa powder

MONKEY BREAD

Makes 4 mini loves

Who doesn't love a great monkey bread recipe? You can make as little or as much as you want, but just know that you will have to adjust your cooking times in your Instant Pot (I made mine in 2 mini loaf pans). The denser the cluster of monkey bread pieces are, the more time you need to add.

Also, when you're assembling your monkey bread into the pans, do NOT press the pieces down into the pans. Just lay them in there. If you push down on them, you are going to create different density issues, and your monkey bread will not cook properly.

Directions

1. In a large bowl or plastic bag, add sugar and cinnamon. Combine well.

2. Cut 4 biscuits in quarters, add to sugar mixture, and coat thoroughly. Place sugar-coated biscuit pieces into 2 mini loaf pans. Repeat the process until your biscuits are used or your pan is full.

3. Add butter and brown sugar into a small bowl, and place in the microwave for 45 seconds. Once butter is melted, stir thoroughly with a fork. Evenly distribute the caramel sauce between the two loaf pans.

4. Add 1 cup of water to your pot and place trivet into the bottom. Place both loaf pans onto trivet, and lightly cover the top of the loaf pans with a piece of foil.

5. Place on Manual High Pressure for 21 minutes, and NPR for 5 minutes then QPR.

Ingredients

½ cup sugar
1½ teaspoons cinnamon
1 can Pillsbury Grands! Southern Homestyle Butter Tastin' biscuits
½ stick butter
½ cup light brown sugar
1 cup water

You'll Need

1 piece of foil

GRANDMA'S BREAD PUDDING

Serves 6

Everyone loves this classic bread pudding for dessert. Sometimes I feel like our grandmothers held a convention about certain recipes that everyone had to make for their family, and this was their number one choice. Everyone has their own way of making them by adding in chocolate chips, butterscotch, and even fresh berries. There's so many different variations you can do with the basic recipe.

Directions

1. In a medium bowl, add all wet ingredients and beat with a fork until well blended.

2. Add in your chopped challah bread and cinnamon, and mix until all liquid is absorbed.

3. Pour contents into your dish.

4. Add 1 cup of water into your pot and place trivet into base. Lightly spray foil with nonstick spray. Place dish onto trivet, and lightly place foil on top of dish. Lock lid and close vent. Cook on High Manual Pressure for 11 minutes.

5. Once done, QPR and remove lid. Allow to sit and cool. You can serve with a little extra sweetened condensed milk on top.

Ingredients

1 egg
¼ cup milk
¼ cup sweetened condensed milk
2 cups chopped and cubed challah bread
½ teaspoon cinnamon
1 cup water

You'll Need

7-cup rectangular Pyrex dish
Aluminum foil
Nonstick spray

STEAMED RAISIN YOGURT "COOKIES"

Makes 1 dozen

These traditional Japanese steamed "cookies" are so divine. These are known as Japanese Yogurt Mushi-pans. They wind up being little cushions of delight that are subtly sweet. The raisins are a great added bonus.

They are traditionally made in ramekins or other small cake molds; however, the dough is very pliable, and I decided to roll them into little cookies. The Greek yogurt gives them a little health boost, and they take no time at all to make and "bake" in your Instant Pot.

The only thing you have to do is to keep an eye on your water level. We are steaming them, and water will evaporate from your machine.

Directions

1. In a bowl, whisk together sugar and flour. Add in oil and yogurt. Mix well with a fork. Gently fold in raisins.

2. Add about a tablespoon of dough to each piece of parchment paper.

3. Add 1½ cups of warm water to your pot. Insert trivet.

4. Place 4 raisin "cookies" in your authentic Instant Pot silicone steamer basket. Place basket on trivet. Lock lid and close vent. Cook on High Manual Pressure for 10 minutes and allow to NPR for 10. QPR any remaining pressure.

5. Remove steamer basket and allow "cookies" to cool.

Ingredients

2½ tablespoons granulated sugar
1 cup self-rising flour
2 tablespoons vegetable oil
½ cup Greek yogurt
¼ cup raisins
1½ cups warm water

You'll Need
Parchment paper cut into 3 x 3-inch squares

POTATO CANDY

Makes approximately 3 dozen pieces

Remember this old-fashioned dessert? This candy came around from the early German immigrants' days. Not everyone could afford the more expensive candy, like chocolates. However, potatoes were everywhere. With a little bit of love, this sweet delicacy came to America and we added our own touch to it: adding peanut butter and rolling it into a swirl.

Directions

1. Place potato in pot and add 1 cup of water. Close lid and lock vent. Cook on High Manual Pressure for 5 minutes. QPR the pressure once done.

2. Drain potato and place in a medium bowl. Use a hand mixer to beat the potato until it is lump-free.

3. Slowly add in all powdered sugar. Once done, place on a large piece of waxed paper lightly coated with powdered sugar.

4. Roll potato mixture out into a ¼-inch thick rectangular shape. Spread the peanut butter evenly on top. Starting at a long side, roll as if you were making cinnamon rolls.

5. Place in the fridge for about 1 hour. Remove wax paper and cut into pinwheel slices.

Ingredients

1 small russet potato, peeled and sliced
1 cup water
8 cups powdered sugar
⅔ cup peanut butter

CARAMEL APPLE PUDDING CAKE

Serves 8

This cake is very autumnal, it's everything that's perfect about the fall weather. People go crazy over pumpkin spice–flavored everything, but I'm all about apple spice. The more the better!

I love making this pudding cake because it doesn't get dried out after making it in your Instant Pot. It stays nice and moist, even a couple of days afterward! Be sure to make this for your next get-together or family gathering. Everyone will simply love it.

Apple Layer Directions

1. Press Sauté on your machine and add butter. Once butter has melted, add in apples and remaining ingredients. Stir frequently. Cook for approximately 5–6 minutes. Press Cancel.

2. Spray mold with nonstick spray. Add apple topping to the bottom of the mold, and set to the side.

Pudding Cake Directions

1. To your pot, add 4 cups of warm water and trivet. Press Sauté and wait for water to boil. Once boil has been reached, press Cancel.

2. In a medium bowl, add flour, salt, baking powder, bread crumbs, cinnamon, and nutmeg. Mix with a whisk until ingredients are evenly distributed.

3. In a large bowl, cream together butter and brown sugar. Once creamed, add in eggs, molasses, and applesauce. Mix well, but don't overmix. Slowly add in your dry mixture to your wet. Folding works best. Once done, pour batter into mold over the apples.

4. Cover mold with foil and crimp edges to remain sealed. Lock lid and close vent. Cook on High Manual Pressure for 45 minutes. Allow to NPR fully (approximately 20–25 minutes). Insert a dry toothpick to see if it's done. If not, then cook for an additional 15–20 minutes and NPR. Allow to cool before serving.

Apple Layer Ingredients

1 tablespoon unsalted butter
2 Granny Smith apples, peeled, cored, and diced
1 tablespoon sugar
¼ teaspoon nutmeg
¼ teaspoon allspice
¼ teaspoon cinnamon

Pudding Cake Ingredients

4 cups warm water
1¼ cups all-purpose flour
Pinch of salt
2¼ teaspoons baking powder
1 cup plain dry bread crumbs
1 teaspoon cinnamon
½ teaspoon nutmeg
1 stick unsalted butter
½ cup brown sugar
2 large eggs
¼ cup molasses
¼ cup applesauce

You'll Need

7-cup pudding mold or similar dish
Nonstick spray
Piece of aluminum foil

DAMPFNUDEL

Makes 1 dozen

I came across this little gem of a dish while doing some research, and am I ever happy that I did! This is a typical dish found in southern Germany. Here's a fun fact for my history buffs: Master baker Johannes Muck and his wife made 1,200 Dampfnudels to feed the Swedish soldiers during the Thirty Years' War.

This is flexible because it is used as either a main course or a dessert. I opted for the dessert route, but I do see myself making this for a delicious hearty soup in the future!

I paired mine with a rich vanilla sauce, but you can use custards, fruits, jams, and more.

Directions

1. Dissolve the yeast and 1 tablespoon sugar in warm water. Let the mixture stand until bubbly. In another bowl, add 1 tablespoon sugar, lukewarm milk, salt, and melted butter. Mix until sugar has been dissolved.

2. Add the yeast mixture to the milk mixture and then add the flour and knead until dough is smooth and elastic (approximately 7–8 minutes). Add flour as necessary, until the dough can be formed into a soft ball.

3. Lightly spray a bowl with nonstick spray and place the dough in it. Allow the dough to double in size. This will take about 1 hour.

4. Once done, punch dough. Remove from bowl and knead for 2 minutes on a lightly floured surface. Divide dough into 12 equal pieces and roll them into balls. Place them in an Instant Pot steamer basket. Side by side is fine; they will all fit. Allow dough balls to rise for about 10–15 minutes.

5. Place 1½ cups of warm water into your pot and place trivet into bottom. Place steamer basket on trivet. Close lid and lock vent. Cook on High Manual Pressure for 40 minutes and NPR. Serve warm or chilled with sauce of your choice.

Ingredients

1½ teaspoons active dry yeast
2 tablespoons sugar, *divided*
¼ cup lukewarm water
¾ cup lukewarm milk
Pinch of sea salt
2 tablespoons melted butter, *divided*
2½ cups all-purpose flour, sifted
Optional: vanilla sauce or sweetened condensed milk for topping

PHILIPPINE STEAMED CAKE (PUTO)

Serves 8

This steamed cake almost has the same versatility as the dampfnudel recipe, in the fact that it is served with both sweet and savory dishes. These also serve as a great snack item if you steam them in individual molds or cupcake holders. You will most definitely find this on almost every table during the holidays.

This batter is very loose, so don't let that scare you. Like a couple of other breads and cakes in this book, this is one that's meant to be eaten within 24 hours of making it. It's a deliciously dense, moist cake that you and your family will definitely enjoy.

Directions

1. In a large bowl, add all dry ingredients and whisk together. In another bowl, add egg whites, milk, and water. With a handheld mixer, beat on medium speed for about 5–6 minutes.

2. Add the wet ingredients to the dry and mix well. Lightly spray your mold with nonstick spray. Pour batter into your mold. Cover mold with foil.

3. Add 2 cups of water into your pot and insert trivet. Place mold onto trivet. Cook on High Manual Pressure for 40 minutes and 10 minutes NPR. Be sure to QPR any remaining pressure.

Ingredients

¼ teaspoon salt
1¾ cups all-purpose flour
1 cup sugar
2 tablespoons baking powder
¼ teaspoon salt
2 large egg whites
¼ cup milk
1½ cups water
7 cup mold
Nonstick spray

You'll Need
Piece of aluminum foil

STICKY TOFFEE CAKE

Makes 4

When it comes to desserts, the sticky toffee cake is my absolute favorite dessert in the entire world. If you know me, you would probably guess chocolate. Nope. It's this cake. It's a traditional English steamed pudding cake made with dates.

I probably love it because it reminds me of my mom's date nut bread. With that being said, this has been served in some of the finest restaurants that I've worked in from Georgia to New Jersey, and everyone always absolutely loves it. I made individual desserts out of this, but you can make one great big cake by using a 7-cup mold. You would have to increase your cooking time, but it will be totally worth trying. This is perfect to serve during the holidays.

Directions

1. In a bowl, cream together butter and sugar until fluffy peaks have formed. Add egg and lightly mix. Slowly add in flour and baking powder—your mixture will look very crumbly at this moment.

2. In a separate bowl, add dates, baking soda, vanilla extract, and boiling water. Mix well. Add this mixture to your other bowl of dough, and incorporate.

3. Lightly spray ramekins with nonstick spray. Distribute dough into ramekins, filling ¾ of the way. Cover each ramekin with foil.

4. Add 1½ cups water to your pot and insert trivet. Place ramekins on trivet. Don't be afraid to stack! Lock lid and close vent. Cook on High Manual Pressure for 30 minutes and allow to NPR for 10 minutes. QPR any remaining pressure.

5. Carefully remove ramekins from your pot. Allow to cool, and then flip onto a plate upside down. Remove ramekin. Serve with your favorite caramel sauce.

Ingredients

4 tablespoons butter, softened
¾ cup sugar
1 large egg, lightly beaten
1 cup boiling water
1½ cups all-purpose flour
1 teaspoon baking powder
1¼ cups pitted dates, chopped finely
1 teaspoon baking soda
1 teaspoon vanilla extract
Caramel sauce
Nonstick spray
4-ounce ramekins
Aluminum foil

Hints, Tips, and FAQs

I hope these recipes have inspired to you to not be afraid of your Instant Pot, and to keep on using for many other recipes you find or ones that you create yourself.

Use the Instant Pot as a tool like you would anything else in your kitchen. It's a great space saver, and it helps you to be able to do other things while preparing a meal for your family or a dessert to be shared.

Questions will probably pop up, though. So, you followed my recipes exactly, and you didn't get the same outcome that I did. We have to try to diagnose what happened along the process—there could just be something small that affected the results, or maybe it wasn't a recipe that you were having an issue with, but the Instant Pot itself. Well, let me see if I can help!

1. Oh No! I pour liquid into my Instant Pot, and now it's all over the counter.
Okay, so you forgot to the metal pot inside before pouring in your contents. *Always* double-check that your pot is in your machine before adding ingredients for a recipe. Does this mean that it's the end of the road for your machine? No, not always. Clean it up really well and allow to fully dry before trying to plug in and use again.

2. My Instant Pot has been on for over 20 minutes, and it still hasn't come to pressure. It's just hissing away and steam is coming out.
This can happen for a couple of reasons.

1. Did you move the vent to the closed position on your lid? If you didn't, no pressure will build up. The steam will just continue to come out of the vent.
2. Did you put frozen food into the pot? If you do, it will take the pot longer to come to pressure, because it is extra cold. It takes a while to get the right temperature to make the steam pressure that is required to get your pot to pressurize.
3. Check your pressure pin on the pot and make sure nothing is clogging the hole. If you're not properly cleaning your machine or giving basic maintenance, then it can

get clogged and the pin will not be able to pop up. Pressurized steam will continue leaving the hole, and your machine will never come to pressure.

4. You forgot to put your silicone ring back into the lid of your pot. This happens more often than you think—if you're cleaning your silicone ring after each usage, you can sometimes forget to put it back in.

5. Let's talk about your machine just not coming to pressure as fast as you thought it would. This can happen from putting in too much liquid into your pot. The more ingredients and liquid that has been added into your pot, the longer it will take to come to pressure.

3. I got a burn notice on my machine. What did I do wrong?

There's a few things that could have gone awry here, but don't fret just yet.

1. You put dairy products into your Instant Pot while cooking. There are plenty of recipes that include dairy products like milk, heavy cream, and cheese. These are more dense than other liquids like stock and water. So they will stay close to the bottom of the pot where the heating element is and the bottom of the pot will start to get a little bit of a charring effect. For the most part, always add dairy in last. That is the general rule of thumb.

2. You didn't have enough liquid in your pot, or you used ingredients that are just too dense, such as crushed tomatoes, tomato sauce, etc.

3. Sometimes it is a user error. If you're following along with a recipe that you found online or in a cookbook, follow the order of ingredients. Cooking in your Instant Pot has a lot to do with layering ingredients in just the right way to make it work. Example: pasta dishes will always have pasta added in last, unless you're making mac and cheese. This is different because you're just cooking pasta in water, and adding other things to it. We spend a lot of time formulating recipes and how we can make them work in the Instant Pot. We make mistakes, but we fix them so other people can enjoy them as we do.

4. Did you put on too much time onto the cooking timer? Always double-check the amount of time you press for each recipe.

4. I want to make a recipe, but I'm not sure how much liquid to put into my pot.

Well, we've all been there! I definitely recommend starting off with 1 cup of liquid. Sometimes you'll need more, but that comes with trial and error cooking in your pot. Once you've become more familiarized with the cooking process, how to handle liquids for various dishes will become second nature.

5. My instant Pot smells so bad. How can I get rid of the smell?

There are a lot of things you can do.

1. One of the first things that I like to do is have 2 different sealing rings for the lid on hand. I use one for savory cooking and the other for my sweets cooking.
2. Cook a couple of russet potatoes in your pot, with the skin on. The skin of the potatoes helps to absorb the smell from the rings. I came across this by accident! You can cook the potatoes on High Manual Pressure for at least 4 minutes.
3. A lot of people wash their rings in the dishwasher or soak them in hot soapy water.
4. Some people swear by throwing in a cup of water with a couple of lemons cut in half. Put it on High Manual Pressure for 5 minutes, and the smell is gone.

6. My recipe is taking longer to cook than yours did!

That's to be expected. We all live in different levels of elevation. The higher your elevation, the longer it will take to come to pressure. This is also true with baking. What can take me 2 hours to let my yeast dough rise, could take you 2½ hours. Don't be afraid to put it back in your pot for a few more minutes! Here's a great cheat sheet to help with cooking times.

If your home elevation is above . . .	increase by . . .	or multiply time by . . .
3,000 feet	5%	1.05
4,000 feet	10%	1.1
5,000 feet	15%	1.15
6,000 feet	20%	1.2
7,000 feet	25%	1.25
8,000 feet	30%	1.3
9,000 feet	35%	1.35
10,000 feet	40%	1.4

7. I have so much liquid coming out of my vent when depressurizing it!

This tends to happen when you overfill your pot. It'll spew ingredients, juices, sauces, and food particles if you're trying to do a QPR when a recipe has finished. If you have a lot of liquid in your pot because you're making a big batch of soup, then slowly and gently QPR. You don't have to turn the valve to the vent open all the way. Put on a silicone oven mitt, and slowly turn the vent open a little bit at a time. This way not everything will come rushing out. I say to use a silicone oven mitt because steam can shoot through a cloth one.

8. Is an instant Pot expensive?

In my opinion, they're not that expensive. I use mine very often, so I get great usage out of it. Many places have them on sale through the year, and the holidays are the perfect time to snag some amazing deals. You will probably have some thrift luck at a yard sale or a Good Will store. Many people have found them there at a greatly reduced price. Check online, and you might be surprised. So many people sell their Instant Pots because they get frustrated with learning how to use it, and get overwhelmed and discouraged. Trust me, I was there too. Take the time to learn how to use it, and you'll soon learn that you might need 2 or 3 more.

9. I haven't used my machine because I'm afraid of it exploding on me!

Okay. I was there too. But know this, you can't remove the lid if it's still under pressure. If you are able to remove it, you must be super strong. There's a lot of pressure in that special little pot. Pay attention to the pin to make sure that your pot is depressurized, and you won't have anything to fear. Double-check that there's not pressure by making sure your vent on the lid is open, and no more steam is coming out. Just know that lid has 10 or more UL Certified proven safety mechanisms to prevent most of the potential issues

10. I know that my machine is depressurized, but the pressure pin won't drop.

This happens sometimes. It means that something might have gotten stuck and it's glued to the sides at the moment. Lightly tap the pin with the back of a butter knife. It should drop. If that doesn't work, try gently pressing on the pin to help it drop. Once you get your lid off, thoroughly clean the pressure pin area for any stuck ingredients.

11. Is there a difference between the Instant Pot and an electric pressure cooker?

Yes, there is! Yes, the Instant Pot is an electric pressure cooker, but it does so much more than that. You can make yogurt, proof bread, make beer, ferment vegetables and fruit, steam, sauté, brown meat, cook rice, use it as a slow cooker, and the list goes on. So it's not just an electric pressure cooker.

12. Does the Instant Pot really cook faster?

Yes and no. When it comes to cooking a succulent roast or pulled pork, it greatly reduces your cooking time and your meat doesn't dry out. However, there are certain foods it doesn't cook faster, like hard-boiled eggs, seafood, pasta, etc.

13. Can I use my Instant Pot as a fryer?

NO! Don't do this. Please. It doesn't meet any safety specifications for being able to fry anything in it.

14. What size instant Pot should I buy?

Great question! There are currently three different sizes that you can purchase: 3-quart, 6-quart, and an 8-quart.

For 2 people or small side dishes, buy a 3-quart.

For family sizes 3–5, buy a 6-quart.

For family sizes 6 or more, buy an 8-quart.

15. Will my 3-quart Instant Pot have the same cooking time as my 8-quart one?

No. There will be different cooking times for any of these 3 sizes. When following a recipe, make sure you know what size Instant Pot that the recipe is using. All of my recipes used a 6-Quart Instant Pot.

16. My pressure-release knob come off. Now what do I do?

Rinse off and put it back in! It's meant to easily pull off to help with the cleaning process. Just be sure it's pushed back in.

15. If I want to double the recipe, do I have to double the cooking time?

No! You just have to add in a little bit more time. The time you add on really depends on the density of the meats and vegetables, and how much extra you're putting in there. Each case is different. If you're doubling up on the vegetables, then you shouldn't have to increase your cooking time at all. It would just take a little bit longer to bring it up to pressure. If you double up on the meat, then maybe add on a few extra minutes. It's very subjective, and you will become more comfortable as you continue using your Instant Pot.

16. My chicken turned out really dry; what's going on?

Well, the thing is that you're probably cooking your chicken in water. Water has no fat or flavor for the chicken. Try using a nice chicken broth, or use chicken breast on the bone with skin on. This will help ensure that your chicken isn't too tough.

The other thing is that you might have cooked the chicken too long in the Instant Pot.

Lastly, I've heard many chefs in restaurants give this hint: Don't cook frozen chicken. Can you do it in the Instant Pot? Of course you can! However, there is always a chance that your chicken might be a little dry.

17. Can I put my Instant Pot on the stove to cook?

Of course you can! Just *please* make sure that the stove isn't on! You'd be so surprised how many people turn on one of the burners by accident, or place their machine on a hot top. It totally melted the bottom of the machines, and a lot of tears were shed.

However, I love using my machine on the stove because of the steam that comes out. The steam released won't damage any of my cabinets from the constant use. If you're done cooking on the counter, carefully move your IP over to the stove to release any pressure into the overhead vent. It works like a charm. You can always get one of the directional steam venters, but Instant Pot doesn't recommend anything that might block the flow of steam that comes out of the IP.

18. Wait. My machine doesn't have a manual button on it. What now?

Don't worry. Different models have different terms. On certain Instant Pot models, it has the phrase Pressure Cook on it.

TYPICAL COOKING TIMES FOR FOOD

If you're in the mood to create your own recipes, then below you will find a rough estimate guide to cooking everything from seafood to meat. These are suggested times that should work out the best for you. This will help put your culinary skills to the test and set you on the path of what you're looking for!

VEGETABLES	PRESSURE in Minutes	(High or Low) *QPR ALL VEGETABLES
Artichokes	4	High
Asparagus	1	Low
Beet, Cubed	4	Low
Bok Choy	7	High
Broccoli	5	Low
Brussels Sprouts	4	High
Cabbage	3	High
Carrots	4	High
Cauliflower	10	High
Cherry Tomatoes	5	High
Chicory	10	High
Collards	8	High
Corn, on the cob	3	High
Corn, in husk	10	High
Eggplant	3	High
Green Beans, fresh or frozen	3	High
Kale	5	High
Leeks	3	High
Mushrooms, dried	10	High
Mushrooms, fresh	5	High
Okra	3	High
Onions	3	High
Parsnips	3	High
Peas, shelled fresh or frozen	1	Low
Peppers	3	Low
Potatoes, baby or fingerling	6	High
Potatoes, chopped	5	High
Potatoes, whole	6	High
Pumpkin, sliced	4	High
Rutabagas	2	High

Squash, Acorn, halved	8	High	
Squash, Spaghetti, Halved	5	High	
Squash, yellow	4	High	
Sweet Potatoes	16	High	
Swiss Chard	2	High	
Tomatoes	3	High	
Turnips, whole	6	High	
Zucchini	3	High	

SEAFOOD	PRESSURE in Minutes	(High or Low)	NPR or QPR
Calamari	18	High	QPR
Carp	6	High	QPR
Clams, fresh	5	High	QPR
Cod	3	Low	QPR
Crab	3	Low	QPR
Haddock	7	Low	QPR
Halibut	7	Low	QPR
Lobster	3	Low	QPR
Mussels	1	Low	QPR
Ocean Perch	7	Low	QPR
Octopus	20	High	NPR
Oysters	6	Low	QPR
Salmon	6	Low	QPR
Scallop	1	High	QPR
Scampi	2	Low	QPR
Shrimp	2	Low	QPR
Swordfish	7	Low	QPR
Squid	4	High	NPR
Tilapia	3	HIGH	QPR
Trout	12	Low	QPR

MEAT	PRESSURE in Minutes	(High or Low)	*NPR ALL MEAT
Beef, brisket	60	High	
Beef, flank steak	15	High	
Beef, ground	7	High	
Beef, Osso buco	25	High	
Beef, oxtail	45	High	
Beef, ribs	60	High	
Beef, roast	40	High	
Beef, round	60	High	
Beef, stew (cubed)	22	high	
Beef, tongue	50	High	
Chicken, (leg, thigh, breast, wings)	14	High	
Chicken Breast, boneless	8	High	
Chicken, strips	1	High	
Chicken, whole	25	High	
Cornish Hen	10	High	
Deer, roast	33	High	
Duck, whole	35	High	
Elk, roast	35	High	
Goat, roast	22	High	
Lamb, Chops	7	High	
Lamb, leg/shank	45	High	
Lamb, roast	25	High	
Lamb, shoulder	25	High	
Pheasant	20	High	
Pork, Belly	40	High	
Pork Chops	7	High	
Pork, loin	15	High	
Pork, roast	35	High	
Pork, ribs	21	High	
Rabbit	18	High	
Veal, Osso buco	28	High	

Again, these are all recommended times. It will help you decide what you want to make, and what ingredients to put together.

You can see that things cook at different times, so you'll be able to add in your other ingredients at different time intervals so they don't overcook.

CLEANING TIPS

1. Clean all of the small parts in your lid. Remove the pressure release by simply pulling it up. There's a small metal "basket" attached to the inside. You can remove that too, by pulling on it. Remove the silicone ring. Wash everything with warm soapy water. You can also put the whole lid into the dishwasher! It won't harm anything.
2. Use Q-tips to clean the inside of the rim of the machine. Try to keep it free of debris and food. This will ensure that your machine will properly seal when pressurizing.
3. Make sure to drain your moisture cup that's attached to the side of your machine.
4. Use a lightly wet washcloth or towel to clean the outside of your Instant Pot.
5. If you use your trivet, don't forget to wash it. No worries! It's dishwasher safe.
6. Using a pipe cleaner or small bristle brush, be sure to wash any and all small parts, areas, and surfaces.

Conversion Charts

Metric and Imperial Conversions

(These conversions are rounded for convenience)

Ingredient	Cups/Tablespoons/Teaspoons	Ounces	Grams/Milliliters
Butter	1 cup/ 16 tablespoons/ 2 sticks	8 ounces	230 grams
Cheese, shredded	1 cup	4 ounces	110 grams
Cream cheese	1 tablespoon	0.5 ounce	14.5 grams
Cornstarch	1 tablespoon	0.3 ounce	8 grams
Flour, all-purpose	1 cup/1 tablespoon	4.5 ounces/0.3 ounce	125 grams/8 grams
Flour, whole wheat	1 cup	4 ounces	120 grams
Fruit, dried	1 cup	4 ounces	120 grams
Fruits or veggies, chopped	1 cup	5 to 7 ounces	145 to 200 grams
Fruits or veggies, puréed	1 cup	8.5 ounces	245 grams
Honey, maple syrup, or corn syrup	1 tablespoon	0.75 ounce	20 grams
Liquids: cream, milk, water, or juice	1 cup	8 fluid ounces	240 milliliters
Oats	1 cup	5.5 ounces	150 grams
Salt	1 teaspoon	0.2 ounce	6 grams
Spices: cinnamon, cloves, ginger, or nutmeg (ground)	1 teaspoon	0.2 ounce	5 milliliters
Sugar, brown, firmly packed	1 cup	7 ounces	200 grams
Sugar, white	1 cup/1 tablespoon	7 ounces/0.5 ounce	200 grams/12.5 grams
Vanilla extract	1 teaspoon	0.2 ounce	4 grams

Oven Temperatures

Fahrenheit	Celsius	Gas Mark
225°	110°	$1/4$
250°	120°	$1/2$
275°	140°	1
300°	150°	2
325°	160°	3
350°	180°	4
375°	190°	5
400°	200°	6
425°	220°	7
450°	230°	8

Index